SUBSEQUENT TO SUMMER

Also by Roy Fuller

Subsequent
to
Summer

ROY FULLER

I have my memories, which are agonies;
Yet many secrets, which were sacred once,
I now care very little to preserve.
Few men remain whose praise or blame I heed;
And so I write about myself with freedom.
My friends and neighbours may throw scorn upon me,
And say that I am too communicative;
But, if my poems should live after me,
Those who survive me will not blame me for it.
What will my readers care for me and mine
Unless I take them to my confidence?

JAMES HURNARD, *The Setting Sun* (1870)

1985

The Salamander Press

The Salamander Press Edinburgh Ltd
18 Anley Road, London W14

First published November 1985

ISBN 0 907540 72 4

Made and printed in Great Britain
Set in Linoterm Baskerville
by Speedspools, Edinburgh.
Printed and bound by Oxford University Press.
Designed by Tom Fenton at the Salamander Press.

Dedication

July has usually gone before the bard
Opens the book where he can truly feign—
Now, in old age, often an old refrain—
And tries to find particulars for hard
Thoughts and soft feelings. Summer's lavish fard
Held far too many elements that disdain
An art that's always trying to explain
Notions its audience mostly disregard.

Brief as autumnal stems hang vivid words.
Art joins dust-gatherers on the endless shelves.
Right-thinking poets place with benevolent elves
Kindly librarians, who will recommend
Even the out-of-fashion when the trend
Regards a rhyme as something for the birds.

Contents

Prelude

My mother's birthday: she could still have been
Alive, a not outrageous ninety-six.

Drops on the reddening leaves, such as depend
In autumn's onset from my old man's nose.

Fixed clouds above the city's building-blocks
And ancient domes: immense miscellanies.

I ceased to write novels fifteen years ago
But find it hard to christen myself a poet.

Also, the title's too embarrassing
To claim. Aren't all the poets merely muffs,

Celebrants of the surrogates for living?
Since I adored youth seems no time at all:

To them it's the change from beauty into nothing.
Great tragedy, existence; worth sitting through.

*

Undoubtedly my playing discs derives
From that maternal mezzo-soprano voice

Whose closest to the classic would have been
Anglican church music as a girl.

In the Debussy string quartet it seems
The players all play more or less at once—

Strange in one usually thought of as possessing
A *pointilliste* touch. Exciting are our dreams

In age: the evidence we've slept, as well
As flabbergasting panes on worlds thought lost.

The moon, a ghost all afternoon, by seven
Is falling in sparkles through still-foliaged trees,

Which where I left my mother, in the north,
Long years ago, must be already bare.

*

The Shosty demi-Forty-eight, abundant
Evidence of the classic in our time;

A challenge to do the simpler thing with rhyme,
And even metres other than iambic.

It comes to me, my mother 'dressing-up'—
Tradition of Vesta Tilley, Hetty King.

There, too, creative masks passed down, even
To generations when I'm gone, who knows?

Has one to live to ninety-six to reap
Full pride in the descendants of one's blood?

And what of mental fear, shaky physique,
That need such powerful drugs to nurture dreams;

And make less than happy those we love—a worse
Effect by far than miniaturising verse?

*

Mild, sunny day; still-copulating flies.
I go outdoors and find the garden wrecked.

A passing breeze brings down the apple-leaves;
Their green, faint mottlings merely on the gold.

Debussy in the formal clothes of Bach—
So characterized are Shosty's Twenty-four.

A few days gone: tonight is All Souls' Night.
My mother died in purgatory, so surely

She's now at rest. My life of affairs, to which
She apprenticed me in youth, continues yet;

Confirming her judgement, so she would have thought.
And even I admit its bounds enlarge—

A girl considered on the Woolwich bus:
Millenia of beauty from the Raj.

*

The consequences of a child, gene-rich:
Sometimes beyond a parent's phantasies.

One thinks of Maxim Shostakovich striking
The notes of his sire's creative solitude;

Almost irrelevant they shared the strangeness
Of tyranny and snow. Today the sky

Confirms Newtonian law, its yellow lost,
Arriving at the eye completely blue;

As from the National Gallery emerge
Modern works, in the shape of foreign girls.

And even yet there seems to open out
A world of heroic or ironic art,

Raising me up from Epicure Mammon's poets,
'The same that writ so subtly of the fart.'

I

Dramatis Personae

An editor gently questions if my life
Will satisfy her questing readership.

I've long anticipated such a crab
Since my quotidian doings took the stage.

Yet what's in art beyond the personal?
Or so I ask myself in my defence.

One sees the boring samenesses for others.
One has some notions for a plot of masks.

But then, a melodrama lacking villains;
Men and women without a moral code?

Tales truthful as the journey to the shops;
Dukes and virgins as well as rhymes and stanzas!

I buy *The Browning Cyclopaedia* in
Oxfam, feeling it better in my care.

Garden Olympics

In the urn a torch has lit the busy-lizzie.
Officious pigeons start some vague proceedings.

The crowded, brightly-hatted nasturtium audience
Raises green parasols against the sunlight.

A far competitor thuddingly puts an apple.
Crouching upon his starting-blocks, the weeder.

A blackbird stutters to its take-off.
A bee on the lavender fails the pole-vault.

The privet's made ready for the coming horses.
Routine dope-testing: wasps seem all unready.

What mighty throw will come from this squat figure,
More arms and legs than most, poised in the circle?

Ants exit from the stadium's many exits;
Search for predictably absent taxis.

3

Fin de Siècle I

Shall I survive into the 'nineties, often
A century's fool-proof period for art?

The harpist's always hopeful to be heard
Above the sawing ranks and piercing breaths.

Evening: a fox turns tail, perhaps alarmed
By the Prom's horn concerto filtering through

Open french windows, for even Richard Strauss
Gives to the *genre* echoes of the hunt.

Tumbler and pen in skilled gripe, thumb-opposed,
What bosh I dream up at the end of day!

—Close to lop-sided Jupiter, who shines
In the more navy-blue than sable sky,

South of the near grey eighteenth-century houses;
Night of warmth, alighting or battering moths.

4

Fin de Siècle 11

As usual, the summer's being squandered—
Season I love, somehow rarely enjoy.

'Thou art not August unless I make thee so'—
But one's no puissant Wallace Stevens, though

Certainly wishing at times in life to be
More of a kidder, not least in poetry.

To lure the fox you must put up with turds
And scratchings on the lawn. Odd, such wild life

Is wildly fascinating to observe—
Maybe to enter, should that rather far

Hazard occur, so as to find myself
Among the sandalwood and chrysolite,

Where 'the bright girls lie panting with their dreams',
And nothing counting in the world but words.

5

Symphonic Dances

Tomato cut in half: wrong-coloured Ace
Of Spades surrounded by exclamation marks.

Having against the odds remembered to
Unplug the lately-charging mower, I

Feel I can now unexpectedly expire
Without undue disaster. In any case,

Low-lying weeds would continue to escape;
Rachmaninov emerge whoever lowered

The stylus in the groove; the pattern, though
Completed, warmingly repetitive.

I wouldn't mind if I were labelled 'the
Composer in D minor'—so I think,

Subsequently supping on a cold
Corpse and some fortune-teller's warning cards.

6

At St Michael and All Angels, Wilmington

I.m. Henry Christian Webster Mason, ob. 30 viii 1984

Old pianists' style, the hands consecutive—
One way of squeezing emotion forth, as faintly

Dubious as lavishing emotion on
Non-human life, or even human life . . .

A little time to spare before the service:
September in the tranquil, green churchyard.

A lichened family vault of local gentry
(But then, dear Harry, you'd been here long years);

Bird noises loved outdoors at home; and now
Arrive our sparse surviving former colleagues.

The crippled verger and the single candle,
Bright coffin—but nothing strange or trivial-seeming

Subtracts from eye-stinging memories of that dour
But staunch and witty Scot; the human redeeming.

7

The September Park

Some crumpled leaves, a mallard's widening wake;
Flower-beds vacant till another spring.

I pick a fir-cone up, think: what's it like?
Asymetrical; hooved its numerous legs.

With their supreme indifference to seasons,
Children play on the bandstand steps, it too

Empty of summer's frogged vermilions
And brass and ebony and silvering.

And a tiny Yorkshire terrier in front of me,
Released from oppressive domesticity,

Rolls on the grass, then frees an adhering leaf
With a lick; also oblivious of time.

—The sort of poem old Allen Tate alleged
I could write with one hand tied behind my back.

8

Returning Aircraft, Late Summer

An aircraft and its alternating lights
On demi-stormy, demi-sunset skies.

But what ensues? With lucky amorous seats,
With deals to add great pluses to their stocks,

For passengers the plots of life progress
—Though risking physical catastrophe.

Yet now we all, however sedentary,
May share the last of these, such are our times.

I dream still the disconcerting dreams of youth
In which the sight or touch of love brings on

Its close; or nightmares equally bathetic
(Which I suppose may also haunt the air)

Of lacking the currency to pay hotels,
And soar with summer moths into the rose.

9

Old Age at Sunset

Spectacular autumnal skies begin
Almost as though erupted once again

The Krakatoa Bridges' sonnets knew
When such convulsions belonged to God alone.

It seems insane so patiently to wait,
Let time stream through us, all too conscious of

The logs (more likely crocodiles) that will
Inevitably sink us, soon not late.

Amazing to be losing full control
Of one's own body, so that parts one thought

Irrelevant may do one down—some cross
Unruly baron in the provinces

Who cuts off a vital way. Or merely the sight
Of boiling clouds on jasper porcelain.

Wolf-rats Etcetera

Tiny dry clusters hang among the leaves—
The lime tree's unexpected fruit, as odd

As in a long piece by Tennyson to do
Really with rich or poor men wooing girls.

The news today: some fellow prophesies
That by the time the human species dies

Through its enormous follies, all too plain,
Earth will belong to murderous baboons

And wolf-rats; with penguins masters of the deep,
Whale-size. But this in fifty million years.

The Laureate in a mere century would have felt
An equal horror at the turns of life,

In spite of nature's annual miracles,
Vouchsafed especially to the short of sight.

Gentlemanly, Ungentlemanly

It seems some house-sized asteroids lurk above,
Though not thought over-likely to land on earth

—A bit of luck I'm not sure earth deserves.
Elgar thought daisies in the Wembley turf

(Perhaps all nature) 'gentlemanly'. I,
Myself, in days of boyhood blessed myself

For being English. No doubt if those mad
Messuages fell they'd fall on foreign parts.

This evening, light prematurely fades, and drums
As sharp as Grieg's or Haydn's bring the rain.

Enough ungentlemanly life to face
Without the violent streets from outer space.

Or so I think, able to sense indoors
The sickly yellow glow that buries all.

12

The Abbey

Only one memorable line (or so
Some critic claims today) in Tennyson's

Wellington Ode. But what about the bit
Where Nelson's bones greet the approaching Duke?

Myself in small degree long years ago
Shared in the mingled cheesing-off and what

Reluctantly one has to christen pride
Of serving with others press-ganged in the Andrew.

Often I pass the Abbey on the bus;
Sometimes am summoned to pay memorial

Respects to mortal poets of the land,
Sharing emotion with the philistines

And the absurdly costumed clerisy . . .
Emerging to our memorable skies.

13

A Case of Time

September on the heath: a rugby game
About to start. Four jolly girls arrive

To cheer on the luckiest numbers of thirteen.
No other watchers, and I myself depart.

Where is my often thought-of masterwork,
The Flora of Blackheath? More to the point,

Where are the notes, the drawings and the lore?
I swipe with my stick a dandelion clock.

Ah yes, indeed, it's all a case of time—
Gazes that fasten, not on hairy thighs

But, more romantically, courageous rucks,
Ignoring patriarchs with roving eyes

That soon are reconciled to looking down
Again where amaranth, or whatever, lies.

14

Iberian Style

There is a sense in which we crave the worst;
Sub-Learian cries to bring the heavens down.

The gutters blocked by pre-autumnal waste,
Rain drills the lawn outside the window-pane.

Indoors, preliminary flourishings,
And coffin-beats to let the dead one free,

Denote the beginning on the radio
Of some guitar piece in Iberian style.

Late seedlings heading for the dying light
Make fragile helices if turned away.

—All telling of a general violence,
While is absorbed what's tamed or can be tamed:

The sun across eight-figure miles: a daughter's
Equally lenient love, and even murder.

15

Art, Life and Time

Lancashire early this century, Wessex in
The last—a not too fanciful resemblance.

Though in my boyhood only human sounds
Rose up from choirs, not Hardy's wheezing bands,

Yet wooing was circumspect, and pregnancies
And births not seldom covert and complex.

So drama went on being hatched behind
The voices purely blent at evensong.

And then from the plots of life the moral vanished;
And sanctions from the psalms, if sung at all—

Announcing an age of happy liberty.
But existence, in the Yankee poet's words,

Continued to contain 'more clouds of grey
Than any Russian play could guarantee'.

16

Death on the Heath

Somewhat melodramatic to think of dying
Here on the heath, with rooks and seagulls crying.

Nevertheless, there comes a Hardyesque
View of my figure, suddenly struck down,

Lone and supine in London's emptiness;
And all I feel I've still to say unsaid.

My father taught me not to be afraid
Of kippers; how with the backbone one was able

To bring out other bones; slide in and lift
The blade to set the opposite bones free.

Of course, had he survived till I was more
Than eight years old he would have taught me more.

The kippers augured well: I still avoid
Choking to death over the breakfast table.

Moth

On the window-sill a moth of silver-grey,
Trunk and antennae curved in tiny death.

At once I think of my long contemplated
Fairy poem, where all's reduced in scale.

Today the *TLS*, in noticing
An Ontario production of the *Dream*,

Speaks so compellingly of Titania's
'Account of the chaos in the natural world'

I have to go and look the passage up.
The Arden edition incidentally

Reminds me that fairy 'Moth' is really 'Mote',
As minute as the rest, like 'Mustardseed'—

Perhaps the reason why in fairyland
There can't in fact be human sight of death.

18

Songs, Early and Late

Michaelmas daisies in the evening gloom
Make now the only novel garden hue,

Except some yellowing and reddening leaves
Still too unnumerous to spread the blues.

Passé, it seems, Freud judged by some today
(Thinking of items that exercise their force

Upon the mind still, even in trivial ways—
That staggering song of Kern's 'They didn't believe me',

That could have been a motto-theme for Freud
And was imprinted on my infancy).

Late flowers sport their washed-out mauves, and bees,
Offered few other choices, visit them

As though hot beds of lavender, their tune
Almost when from the crimson folds of June.

19

The Choice

Some pregnant notion in the night occurs,
Even its rhythmic phraseology,

But I'm too indolent to write it down,
And now, ill-spared, it's for ever lost to mind.

I try to cheat bad memory with this,
The record of forgetting's very act,

Since there are sanguine times when anything
Can act as surrogate in art—a sense

The mundane world confirms, for over breakfast,
The morning after, I read in *The Times* about

A wildlife seminar where the Forestry
Commission regretted luncheon guests were given

A choice of venison, or squirrel pie.
Nice, too, some act as gormlessly as I.

Dimensions

The spider, cunningly cocooned all winter
In a corner of the bathroom, never woke.

One can't help feeling envious in a way.
The eyrie goes on getting blacker: who

Will dare to pull it down? I read that infants
On a glass floor will never hesitate

To crawl across a chasm. Shall we thus
Go into our eternal bathroom coign?

From the same text it seems the cosmos is
Symmetrical in some fine, abstract sense.

I've never doubted my affinity
In the natural world with even the grotesque;

Prepared to die in no more dimensions than
Three bathroom planes, chasms irrelevant.

Is God a Mathematician?

A plethora of abstract algebras.
Where do unusual girls get clothes to match

Their looks—such as these narrow drab-green cords
That elongate the elongated legs?

Does mathematics, describing reality,
Possess unreasonable effectiveness?

Whence comes authority for poetry
To claim its relevance to human life?

One really knows, alas, the enormous worlds,
Escaping, exploding, have little to do with us,

Though possibly obeying the rules of reason.
The masses think art a pain to be avoided;

Yet algebraists invent their algebras
Simply to play with: as poets poetry.

22

Kinship

The spiders start arriving in the house.
September's end: yet life's by no means over.

There's the eternal ambiguity
Of whether immigrants come to live or die.

It's not a vixen's ceaseless hunger one
Feels kinsip with (though some might well do so),

Rather her snow-tipped tail, the collarless
Life among housed and collared canine kin,

Or the reveried crossing (as I've seen her make)
Of the sodium crossroad to the mad A2.

Kinship? The piercing of a metal bomb
To make a fizzy mix for my sundowner?

Hearing Rachmaninov compel four hands
To utter lovers' sighs in spiced C minor?

23

In the Park

A pretty girl; walks badly. Almost a précis
Of character. A not so pretty girl;

Limps, brilliant eyes. Perhaps more words required.
A tricycle named 'Bullet' takes its time

To allow me entry to the park. On this
I speak to the driver, with lost irony.

Some girls now dress as though preparing for
Ju-jitsu : precaution needless in my case.

Robins confirm their will to sing again;
The autumn crocus burns its jet of gas

Deep in the heather. Humans lay out their parks
And put on vainly shape-disguising garbs

With what intent but art I'd like to know—
If art can triumph over slouch and eyes.

24

Pawmarks

Unfair to make fun or light of death when one's
Alive with negligible agony.

Death's harbingers will choke the jesting back,
As well one knows from art and life. I see

Across the bonnet of a fellow's car
The dried-mud footprints of a cat, and want

To tell him how exasperating yet
Endearing the phenomenon, although

Expect he knows this well. Quite heavily
There hangs the burden on the busybody

Poet of a lifetime's dead or intruding cats
And other debts he never will discharge;

Not least, recording the awful change from love
And observation to sick indifference.

25

Spirits

Some ghosts lurk in the night-time garden—ours,
Or so it fancifully seems. Shall I

Bring in the washing, or risk autumnal rain?
For weeks I've played a Dvořák string quartet

As part of writing's evening ritual.
What monstrous musicality! Moreover,

Those works got better as the years went on;
No need to keep his spirits up with spirits.

All that has happened in Europe's heart within
My life—the wars, the frontiers changing, hope

Successively extinguished and relit—
Vague with the booze and music rises up.

Quite insubstantial in the temperate air,
The pallid waifs or refugees look in.

26

Twilights

Astounding early night of late September—
Completely cloudless and still starless sky;

Though one orb hanging yellow in the south.
Presumably it's still the 'civil' twilight,

Preceding the 'nautical' (the terms I learn
From *The Times* monthly feature on the heavens).

Yes, soon I see some points of light appear:
About as far off as my Navy days!

Guarding a hut from spies (the enemy
Also light-years away), or gazing from

A trooper's deck, I surely failed to watch
The approach of night-times as a poet should.

And even now I move indoors too soon,
To prove my Navy pals were aptly Scotch.

27

At Hextable School

A visit to the sixth form of a school.
What can be said that's any use but 'Read'?

It is the poet draws the bonuses—
The drive along the bypass, bringing back

Far memories, and getting up the revs,
A change from the well-worn, costive tracks of town;

Equal exchanges with a generation
I could with ease grandfather; and the teacher's

Sparing for me his service to the young.
I daresay angularities will mellow,

Surrounding nature heal the carved-out site.
In other words, the heart is hooked, for once—

Through flattered self-esteem, or trust the nation
Is after all in decent hands, who cares?

28

Calm

The brilliant fragile sunshine, fragile calm:
Miraculous first tea-time of October.

The winy smell, the wasps dissatisfied
With plenitude like spoiled brats of the rich.

Crunching the windfalls underfoot brings back
That line in poor old Isaac's 'Dead Man's Dump'.

As lucky to last a season as a war—
Or so it seems, alarming decades on.

Where are the closely following isobars
That may be expected at this time of life?

Hard to believe in destiny relenting
Even for uneventful afternoons—

Detaching fruit the size of childish breasts
As poignantly as severing love in dreams.

29

Nagging Fears

Fiction reviews, on which my eye alights—
Massage parlours, vast intake of booze,

Output of vomit, Sta-Tite Maxi-Pads,
Blonde with real wings, and mammoth bum and bust.

My heart sinks, then at once revives a bit—
At least I haven't got to read the stuff.

And so autumnal publishing begins.
Tomatoes ripen on the window-sill,

But they're so green and thick-skinned there must be
A nagging fear the thing may not come off.

Which makes me realise the other fear
Has not quite gone—the treason of the clerks

And all that guff. No comfort in the thought
Time was required in millions for the eye.

30

Earlier and Later Days

Driving, the light of five o'clock still shines
Through leaves, and dazzles intermittently.

Such lingering metaphors of summer bring
Sensations back, somehow, of earlier days.

Entering the house, I see on the TV screen
Two chaps discussing a mysterious thing.

'What's that?' I ask at once. She even more
Mysteriously replies: 'False tongues of wolves.'

The motor car's been garaged nice and dry
(Desirable in its state of body rust),

Discharged the unusual chores away from home;
A drink or two by no means premature.

'False tongues of wolves?' A staggering turn to life.
'For horror films.' As ever, down to earth.

31

The Powers

The chestnuts are ejected by the tree
So vigorously I'm surprised, and stay,

Like a village smithy, under the spreading boughs.
Obeying some dictate of geometry,

The husks split in a zig-zag, show inside
A cleanness not excluding stains of birth.

And as the fusillade goes on, I see
The progeny's force derives from gravity—

Comparatively weak, most enigmatic
Of all the powers that rule the universe.

How lucky to be able to describe,
Even withstand, the sniping of the gods

From their elysian, cerulean attic
Well represented by the October sky!

Serials, Old and New

'To be continued in our next'—the legend
Promised more thrills or heart-ache in my youth.

Yes, but one then was on the receiving end—
Not doubting the creator's powers or life.

Sixty years on it's best to leave a note
To stimulate one's own next day instalment,

Otherwise heroines may well cry out
In vain, lashed to the drumming railway lines;

And in the life department one must be
Assiduous in swallowing the pills

For thyroid, heart and water, sovereign thrones—
Not counting those to compensate for sleeping

But intermittently, like a thermostat,
And scarcely sound enough for ancient weeping.

33

Wallace Stevens at Greenwich I

With thanks to William Boyd

'The lines are straight and swift between the stars'
WALLACE STEVENS, 'Stars at Tallapoosa'

Suppose that somehow Greenwich were Tallapoosa.
Suppose iambics could be written here

That didn't hold an awful lot of meaning
Yet went on echoing through the reader's head

And being chanted, after the author dead.
Would one require to be no Englishman

But Pennsylvania Germanian?
Though surely on the meridian we own

A right to lines between the stars, and hence
(If such things must be drawn) this very night

The saucepan of Ursa Major's hanging by
Its handle, rather characteristically

Suburban by the lines of Wallace Stevens,
That one must in the end admit make sense.

34

Wallace Stevens at Greenwich II

At Tallapoosa there are only two
Varieties of day—sunshine or rain.

But here you sometimes can't tell rain from shine.
The day begins with rain, then from beneath

Lights itself up, the sky remaining grey.
They've filling-stations in Tallapoosa too,

It seems, where bunting doubtless hangs as still
As now it hangs just off the Dover road,

But very likely brighter. Were he here,
Stevens would note the new cat in a new

Location—porch-roof, brinded as in *Macbeth*—
Though might transform it to a grander cat

Circling the statue of the liberator
Of Tallapoosa in a crisp atmosphere.

35

Fame at Last

For Julian Symons

Bringing to mind some parallel of art,
You phone, old friend, and say a chap proposes

To wait on you and get your autograph,
Giving as guarantee of faith my name.

Is it a con, or does he really want—
Already half way there—our monikers?

I summon up remembrance of the day
When at the door I wrote what someone wished.

My goodness, have we in our seventies
Achieved sufficient fame at last? The thing,

I expect, comes as a less surprise to you
Whose prose persona has a following.

For me, it's mainly friendship and a voice,
As in some ancient verse from the Chinese.

36

The Squab 1

Chance confrontation: woodlice skulking back
Of the lavatory cistern. Now another

Life has arrived indoors, attended by
Even more fears for the cowardly.

I found a squab expiring in the lane;
Brought it to live with woodlice, if it could.

Perhaps the dauphin of the collared doves
Heard even now proclaiming 'Gogo the Sixth'.

It seems deformity or babyhood
Prevents it from more than sucking a little milk;

Though later, when a squeaking has emerged,
The corrugated bill attacks my hand

Holding some futile product of humankind,
And braves the pity that would make it mute.

37

The Squab 11

It died in accordance with my secret wish.
And now the lavatory deodorant

Goes on reminding of its weekend stay;
The gingery hirsuteness of its birth

Lingering likewise above the plumage, still
More quill than feather, so the small, hard head

Seemed to set out on a level close to death.
Nameless, not far from unknown being, we

Had nonetheless profound connections on
This unique world of a frigid universe.

And pondering the mysteries, it seems
Little more strange you came, my sibling, from

The egg than I directly from the bourne
Of passsion, equally mythical and bizarre.

38

Corporate Luncheon

The tail-coated banqueting *maître d'hôtel*
Proffers a napkin round potato crisps.

I wave the thing away, but later think
That they were very likely rather good,

Far above even the packets sold by Marks,
The venue being a room at the Savoy.

Not many chances now remain to try
The delicacies of the Baghdad of the West,

Being, as I am, merely a year or two
From total superannuation. I

Seem to myself more than a bit *blasé*.
Though if this is giving up the world, declining

To sully scotch and soda with sliced, fried spuds,
No monstrous hardships wait for me hereafter.

39

The Bricklayers' Arms Development

My driver takes me home a funny way,
Not down, but parallel to, the Old Kent Road.

What's this, behind a broken fence? I ask.
'The Bricklayers' Arms development'—an almost

Occult phrase, denoting space and weeds.
Perhaps inspired by bureaucratic sloth,

The land is sinking back to rest among
An otherwise unbroken bricklayers' crust.

I guess the city purlieus of the past
Commonly held poets speculating on

Their ancestors and scions, driven round
(If they were lucky) by knowledgeable slaves—

A pastoral tradition, often augmented
By flocks cropping the grass between the stones.

40

Profiles

An eagle-nose, gouged nostril, sober suit—
I thought that it was T. S. Eliot

Stooping to brush his boots in the Athenaeum
Bog; and, what's more, sufficiently decrepit

To make survival possible today.
A double-take required. That lunch was so

Prolonged I coincided, bound for home,
With schools released from literature to life.

Fond sight considers nose and brow, and finds
Them Greek; the eye a flecked stone until now

Hidden by seas. How strange to note that down
Curls on a cheek; and later from my terrace

Silver sandbanks of a massive shore
Diagonally drift across the moon.

41

Re-election

I come up for re-election to the Board
Of the old Woolwich; special wording, since

I can't according to our rules see out
The usual three years. Though other rules

Are surely more than likely to cut me short.
And someone well might pertinently say

At the AGM: 'Why don't you always rhyme?'
The little flies get in abandoned drinks:

For here I am in October's early days
Anticipating the drama of mid-December.

But why abandon drinks? Here's to the present!
Already more than half retired, I grow

Used as a surgeon to the sight of blood,
Beside the creeper in former office hours.

42

Literary Associations

Sometimes I can't help thinking: what a waste
If after my demise I were to be

Regarded as rather good, since I should quite
Have liked a modicum of celebrity,

Though now the thing's comic more than otherwise.
Besides, obscurity is all one can

Expect, travelling for preference along
The byways of a Tallapoosa, where

I see a still-wet trickle from a post,
Coloured, no dog in sight. There comes to mind

A range of references from literature—
Kafka and Konrad Lorenz to Sherlock Holmes.

A thrilling life! even my faithful few
Readers may well sardonically pronounce.

43

Anatomy of a Cat

Yes, it seemed camouflaged, that brinded cat:
One eye as if completely absent, tail

In several pieces—the squatting shape blocked out
In black and tan and white, appropriate for

Witches' familiar. I don't believe
The cat in *Macbeth* a simple tabby as

The commentaries imply. 'Brinded' is burnt—
In patches—charred, inflamed, exposing bone.

That Wittgenstein thought little of the Bard
I see's to be discussed in some review,

Although experience shows it doesn't do
Even to pass points over in the text—

Much as one wants to trust philosophy
From an old deckchair in a Cambridge room.

44

Landscapes

As if it stood in some vast English park
The chestnut at my modest entrance gate

Is detailed and embrowned according to
The lessons learnt and taught by landscapists.

'Don't fear the obvious' is what one gets
From Liszt as well, artist some come to late

In life. The spider hesitates before
Stepping from charcoal carpet to oatmeal rug.

In parks, the eye will recognize with slight
Surprise a distant stretch of water as

A different element, brushstrokes bold if brief
In dullest grey and silver. Switzerland

Performed for Liszt what less dramatic scenes
Keep going suburban poet, cautious bug.

45

Coming Winter

A pigeon sometimes hesitates in flight,
Or seems to, though perhaps not checking speed.

The radio: Monteux at eighty-four
(Tape of live concert I hear in '84)—

Erratic, passionate, pigeon-type *rubato*,
The Boston band by no means all together.

Outside, the tranquil, dry October weather
Seems only to make more dire the certainty

Of storms on land, in lungs. Though suddenly
One sees that Beethoven is full of songs.

A major portion of the race of birds,
Not fearing the journey down the hemisphere,

Has nevertheless intended to endure
An after all not utterly songless season.

46

Spinning in October

Wisely the spider spins among the sedum;
If wise the fattening of the arachnid race.

A bee can sometimes be released, but flies
Seem at this season too minute for rescue.

Those must include the flies already saved
From drowning by not neglecting garden drinks.

Casadesus' recording of *'Miroirs'*—
Possessed for years, today still yields surprise;

Not through the player playing from the tomb,
But always my hearing it when writing verse—

Verse that has never made me fat, nor will.
Do we die happier in scotch, or more

Diluted vermouth? I marvel freshly, too,
At the amazing pleasures of the human.

47

Indian Love Lyric

Arithmetic flourished with the Hindus, I
Remember in the post-office (which also

Subsumes colonial history of late).
But anyway I wouldn't think to challenge

The sepia girl about the teasing mix
Of packet, airmail lettercards, and stamps.

Later, I see a single curled red leaf
Fortuitously brought or blown indoors.

It makes the occidental carpet seem
Like pavements of Kashmir—or so I dream,

My fancy stimulated by the grille,
Frustrating as purdah. In the former heart

Of empire, autumn provides a surrogate
For her great vassal's lotus-buds, or such.

48

Inspiration

I worried over living quarters for
My fallen fledgling pigeon, brought indoors.

But finally the notion came to me:
Not too much niceness in a pigeon's nest.

After an interval of many years
I spin an Opus 59 quartet.

When all is said and done, of likes and hates,
Testy chords and the rest, the chap could write.

Here adumbrated is the manner of
The great last works; and sublimated passions—

Perhaps for creatures low-scaled as the dove.
Although it's said the starry sky inspired

The *adagio*—as the stars at Tallapoosa
Raised Stevens' sights above the filling-stations.

49

Domestic Interior

A hat-brim cuts into a picture-frame
Within the picture-frame of a Vermeer.

And no-one is looking at a dish of fruit
The Dutchman eyed so narrowly before.

What signifies the everyday in art?
(And what, indeed, the everyday in life?)

Some image, of resemblance but more true,
Must be pinned down, so much depends on means

To trace even the spirit's silhouette.
Thus music makes his poetry to the poet

Disappointing; its arithmetic,
Let alone melody, rudimentary

Beside those infinitely halving strings.
And painters transfiguring geometry.

Coda

Like some crisp eatable, long chestnut leaves
Roll noisily across suburban floors.
Cold, negligible still, is picking clean
The deciduous forests of a hemisphere;
A process that may possibly show up
In images relayed from the satellite,
Puzzling the mighty powers' intelligence.

So on bare twigs rain gathers like a tear,
Shed for the wreckage of imperial August
Rather belatedly, like many tears.
It seems old age increasingly perceives
The emblematic, though even more desires
To absorb the detail—the departing face.
Acorns are grained as is the covert trunk.

A don from the antipodes (where spring
Just starts) writes asking if I read in youth
Turgenev, and what effect it had;
And so reminds me of lands where from the north
The snow already scurries like our leaves.
A house light is switched on, shines out, and makes
A stunning square-cut emerald of the lawn.

Here earth's still in a key not too remote
From F sharp minor, as it were—Scriabin's
Favourite. And if one's surprised to learn
He owned one, that was after all before

The global wars—time of my infancy.
If we could look to art and history,
As well as seasons, for a return of key!

Do we march forward to the enemy
Or (perhaps pretty much the same) crouch round
The camp-fire with our hooch and beans until
An arrow or, more likely, torture comes?
Death is a 'fold' catastrophe, I read,
A cliff-edge fall quite irreversible;
War's a mere 'cusp'. Or was before the Bomb.

Thus prompted, I may re-read Turgenev—
In the happy interlude of print before
Tackling the white hours of the night—and so
Bring back my days of innocent dissidence
When I shared modestly that generous
And pure desire of Red conspiracies
For children to triumph over want and snow.

Has seven decades' passing made earth's rulers
A cast of villains (with a chump or two)?
And what the author of the present work?
A seven-gilled shark laboriously trained
To breathe pentameters? Are life and verse
Games of 'imperfect information', as
It's said; victory only in the card of chance?